W9-BCI-656

> 15.95

DATE DUE

BIKING

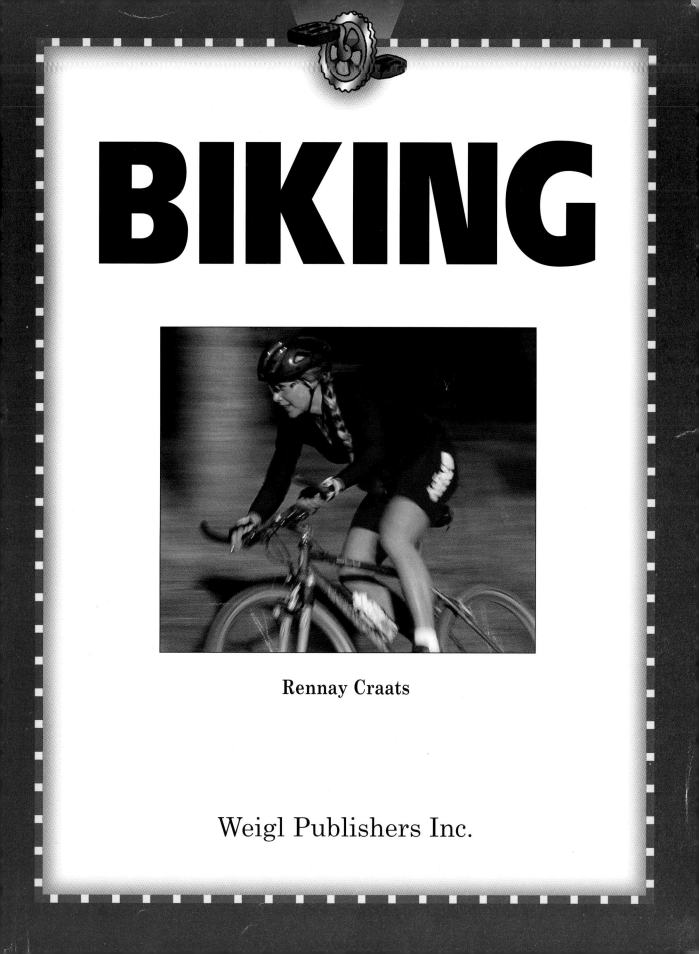

Rennay Craats

Weigl Publishers Inc.

Published by Weigl Publishers Inc.
123 South Broad Street, Box 227
Mankato, MN 56002
USA
Copyright © 2002 Weigl Publishers Inc.
Web site: www.weigl.com

79.6.6
Cr'q
C.1
15.95
2003

Managing Editor
Kara Turner
Layout and Design
Warren Clark
Terry Paulhus
Copy Editor
Jennifer Nault

Library of Congress Cataloging-in-Publication
Data available upon request from the publisher.
Fax: (507) 388-2746 for the attention of the
Publishing Records Department.
ISBN: 1-930954-12-3

Printed in the United States of America
1 2 3 4 5 6 7 8 9 05 04 03 02 01

Photograph credits
Cover: Eyewire; Comstock SportsView: page 7;
Corbis Images: page 1, 4, 5T, 8L, 9, 13B, 16T, 20B,
22; Empics Sports Photography: page 5B, 6, 10, 12,
14T, 15, 16B, 17T, 17B, 18L, 18R, 19L, 19R; Eyewire:
3, 11, 13T, 14B, 20TL, 20TR, 23B; PhotoDisc Ltd:
page 8R, 21, 23T.

Contents

What is Biking?

People have been riding bicycles for more than 150 years. As technology improved, bicycles became more advanced. By the 1960s, cycling was a popular activity for children as well as adults. With the new gearshift, riders were able to cycle off-road, but thin tires made it difficult in some areas. Many riders wanted to explore **rugged** areas on their bicycles. BMX bicycles were soon created. These low, thick-tired bicycles could withstand any **terrain,** but they were not great for climbing hills because they only had one gear. In the 1970s, a group of cyclists in California began taking parts from one bicycle and adding them to parts of others. They used lighter materials and added many gears. The mountain bike was born.

The "Ordinary" bicycle had a large front wheel. It was first produced in 1871.

By 1983, companies across the country were making mountain bikes based on the California models. Today, mountain bikers can cycle on city streets as well as challenging mountain trails. Mountain bikes are made to absorb the shock of riding over bumpy terrain. As the slopes become steeper, bikers gear down to make pedaling easier. Some cyclists ride their bicycles to school or work rather than driving or taking public transit. They may never take their mountain bikes off paved roads or trails. Other cyclists want to discover nature. They enjoy taking their bicycles off-road, riding over rocks and through forests. Some mountain bikers enter off-road competitions and compete in cross-country or downhill races. Mountain bikes have made cycling an entirely different sport.

Cycling first became popular after the invention of the air-filled tire in 1888. Tires help to give a smoother ride when cycling over rough ground.

CHECK IT OUT

To find out more about mountain biking and bike trails, visit
www.imba.com/kids/index.html

Getting Ready to Ride

To participate in mountain biking, some basic equipment is needed. The sport can be dangerous, so riders need to take **precautions**. Proper safety gear can help prevent injuries. With the right equipment and training, mountain bikers can ride faster and farther.

A helmet is a must for riders. It should fit snugly and be comfortable to wear.

Sunglasses protect riders' eyes from the harmful effects of the sun. They also protect the eyes from dust or other particles that can be flicked up while cycling.

Serious bikers wear tight-fitting clothing. The clothes are often made from stretchy materials, such as nylon and Lycra. Less serious mountain bikers usually wear street clothes—T-shirts and comfortable shorts or sweat pants.

The bicycle itself is the most important piece of equipment. Most mountain bikes are made from light metals, such as aluminum, carbon fiber, or **titanium**. Mountain bikes weigh from 20 to 28 pounds, while road-racing bikes weigh from 16 to 20 pounds. Wheels on a mountain bike are relatively small to keep mountain bikers close to the ground for better control and stability. The tires on mountain bike wheels are wider than road-racing tires and have more space between **treads**. More of the tire touches the ground for better **traction**.

Mountain bike handlebars are straight so riders sit upright. This allows them to see the trail ahead. To stop, riders squeeze the brake levers on the handlebars.

The bicycle chain fits along the teeth of the chainring, which is connected to the pedals. It goes around a piece called the freewheel. This is attached to the back tire. As riders pedal, the chain moves the freewheel and the tire spins.

Where to Ride

Mountain bikers are limited only by their imagination. They can ride almost anywhere. Many mountain bikers choose to ride on city trails and streets. They must obey the rules of the road, just as vehicles do. They also need to ride responsibly on trails, as many other people walk, cycle, or inline skate on these paths. There are many national parks for mountain bikers to enjoy. These areas offer bikers a chance to ride off-road in natural areas. There are often hikers or horseback riders sharing the trails. Cyclists need to be considerate of these people by giving them the right of way and riding with control.

Most neighborhoods have bike paths for riders to follow.

Many local and state parks open their trails to bikers.

CHECK IT OUT

For a closer look at the sport, take a peek at

www.extreme.nas.net

epending on where cyclists live, they may have the opportunity to try different kinds of mountain biking. Some adventurous riders enjoy winter riding. Snowy trails provide a challenging workout. Riders must make sure they dress in layers to stay warm. Other riders prefer the challenge of sandy areas, or dunes. Still others like to tackle the steepest hills they can find. Some ski hills allow bikers to ride the slopes in the summer. Mountain biking can take riders nearly anywhere they want to pedal. Riders need to be sure that the area is not private property or a no-cycling zone before setting out.

Warm clothing and gloves make a ride in the snow more enjoyable.

Rules of Competition

Different rules govern different types of mountain biking events. In the observed trials, riders make their way through a course filled with obstacles. It takes balance and control to win this event. Riders aim to finish the course with the lowest number of penalties as possible. A score of zero is a perfect ride.

Cross-country racing involves climbing steep hills and racing down them as well. Many riders compete at the same time, so riders need to race safely. Pushing or leaning on other riders during a race can result in penalties. Riders must stay on the track. Any rider who tries to take a shortcut is **disqualified**.

A competitor in the cross-country event at the 2000 Sydney Olympics stays low and keeps pressure on the brakes to control his speed.

For riders who want the thrill of speed, downhill racing is a great event. The only rule in this competition is to be quick. Downhill racers pedal down a dirt track, and the first to finish wins. The dual slalom is another racing event. This competition requires two cyclists to ride through two identical courses at the same time. The course has several gates that riders must pedal through. Riders are penalized if they miss any of the markers. The cyclist who rides around all the markers and crosses the finish line first wins the race.

Riders should check their tire pressures regularly. The recommended pressure is usually 40 pounds per square inch.

Biking Moves

Many people learn to ride a bicycle when they are young. Riding a mountain bike involves some extra skills. Turning, for example, requires more than just moving the handlebars. Riders need to lean in the direction they are turning. The sharper the turn or the faster they ride, the more they need to lean. Fast riding means cyclists also need to know how to stop. The left brake controls the front brake, and the right brake controls the back brake. To stay balanced, riders lean back and keep their bodies low while braking.

Experience teaches cyclists when to use which gears. Lower gears allow riders to pedal faster. This makes it easier to climb steep hills. Higher gears make for tougher pedaling. These are used for control when traveling downhill. Cyclists must be pedaling when changing gears. Riders must also learn to shift their weight to make uphill or downhill cycling easier.

CHECK IT OUT

To learn more riding tips, surf to
www.wildgoose.com/mtbmain.htm

On long climbs, riders use lower gears and move their weight forward.

The front brakes are stronger than the back brakes. A rider risks a **faceplant** if he or she uses only the front brakes when biking downhill.

S ome areas are too tough to ride through. Riders must pick up their bikes and carry them to easier terrain. To do this, riders put one arm under the top bar and rest the bicycle on their shoulder. Then they hold the handlebars to keep them steady, and stand to lift the bike. The free hand is used to move obstacles, such as branches, out of the way, and for balance.

Riders also need to learn to avoid obstacles. To do this, they steer toward the obstacle at first and then quickly lean to one side to move around the obstacle. Other riders choose to go over obstacles rather than around them. This is called log-hopping. Cyclists log-hop by riding quickly and then leaning back while pulling the front wheel off the ground. When the back wheel is about to contact the obstacle, riders shift their weight forward, drawing the back wheel up. To cross ditches, cyclists ride into the ditch at an angle. As they come out of the ditch, they lean back and keep their bodies low on the bike.

If the going gets tough, mountain bikers carry their bikes. This is hard work, so it is only done for short distances.

Amateur to Pro

Many cyclists begin mountain biking as a hobby. People of all ages can enjoy a bike ride. Other cyclists use biking as a way to get where they need to be. For those cyclists who enjoy the challenge of competition, there are many contests and races to enter, on mountain bikes or on road-racing bikes.

In 1983, the National Off-Road Bicycle Association (NORBA) was created. Today, it has over 30,000 members. It hosts the National Mountain Biking Championships. World Championships are held in Europe and the United States. Athletes can compete in downhill, uphill, or cross-country races. Other contests require cyclists to ride through a course full of obstacles. All of these events challenge the **endurance** and strength of the rider.

Alison Dunlap wins both road and mountain bike competitions. Here, she is competing in a road race.

Every year, NORBA issues permits for more than 1,000 off-road races nationwide.

14

As mountain bikers improve and win competitions, they may decide to try out for regional or national teams. Many work to earn a place on the Olympic team. The Olympic Games offer several different categories for cycling. Some cyclists compete in road races or on tracks. Mountain bikers compete in the cross-country event. For women, this race is between 18.6 and 24.9 miles long. For men, the distance is between 24.9 and 31.1 miles. The race takes competitors across fields, and along forest roads and paths. The first rider across the finish line claims the gold medal. After taking part in the Olympics, mountain bikers can attract **sponsorship** and compete professionally around the world.

David Juarez, riding for the U.S. team, concentrates on biking over rocky ground in the cross-country event at the 2000 Sydney Olympics.

CHECK IT OUT

Find out more about NORBA at
**www.usacycling.org/corp/
?documents/norba.html**

Radical Racing

BMX racing is a popular sport. "BMX" stands for bicycle motocross. Riders copy many tricks from gas-powered dirt-bike riders. BMX bicycles are low to the ground and have thick tires. They are sturdy enough to survive the sport's rough landings.

BMX races can take place inside or outside. The dirt tracks riders race on are usually 700 to 1,300 feet long. Hills and dips are built into the course as obstacles. Riders race around sharp corners and over challenging jumps. This can be dangerous. Because all of the riders race at the same time, one fallen rider can cause several others to fall as well. Riders all know how to fall and how to get out of the way. Most of the time, they can avoid serious injuries. Professional BMX riders receive sponsorship and tour the racing circuit throughout the country and around the world. Many mountain bikers were trained in BMX racing.

The bars on BMX wheels are called pegs and are used when performing tricks.

BMX racers need to keep balanced as they jump in order to control their landings.

The first Tour de France was held in 1903. In 2001, 180 riders racing for twenty teams covered a total distance of 2,164 miles.

Road racing is another exciting cycling sport. It uses many similar mountain biking skills, but a road bicycle has downward-curving handlebars, thin wheels, and a very light frame. Road racers can compete in many different events, including time trials, one-day events, stage races, and track races. In time trials, riders cycle as fast as they can from one spot to another. They race against the clock, and the fastest time wins. One-day events last from 4 to 7 hours and cover between 100 and 175 miles. The Olympic road race is a one-day race. Stage races can last for weeks and span thousands of miles. Each day's race is a stage of the competition. The rider with the lowest overall time wins. The Tour de France is the most famous stage race.

Track racing is an exciting part of road racing. It is held in a stadium called a **velodrome**. The oval track is made of wood or concrete. It has steeply-banked corners that allow cyclists to ride very quickly. Athletes can reach speeds of 67 miles per hour. Sprints, time trials, and team races are held in velodromes.

Track cyclists compete on special bicycles built for speed. Athletes wear helmets and clothing designed to help them go faster.

CHECK IT OUT

To learn more about the exciting sport of BMX, visit

www.bmxtreme.com

Superstars of Today

Biking superstars make the sport even more exciting to watch.

ALISON DUNLAP

BIRTH DATE:
July 27, 1969
HOMETOWN:
Colorado Springs,
Colorado

Career Facts:

- Alison began cycling when she was 19 years old.
- Cycling can be dangerous. In 1994, Alison separated her shoulder and broke three teeth in a crash.
- Alison competed in the 1996 and 2000 Olympic Games. She finished seventh in 2000.
- In 2000, Alison won both the USCF National Cyclo-cross championships and the SuperCup Cyclo-cross Series.
- Alison was the top U.S. rider at the World Mountain Bike Championships in Spain, in 2000.

DAVID JUAREZ

BIRTH DATE:
March 4, 1961
HOMETOWN:
Los Angeles,
California

Career Facts:

- David was originally a BMX racer. He started cycling in 1986.
- In 1995, David won a gold medal at the Pan American Games.
- David is a three-time national cross-country champion. He is ranked number one overall in the senior men's category on the professional men's World Cup circuit.
- David was a member of the 1996 and 2000 U.S. Olympic cycling team.
- Many people know David as "Tinker." He got the nickname as a young boy, and it stuck.
- David trains 28 hours each week and covers about 400 miles on his mountain bike.

LANCE ARMSTRONG

BIRTH DATE:
September 18, 1971
HOMETOWN:
Plano, Texas

Career Facts:

- At just 16 years of age, Lance was a professional **triathlete**.
- In 1993, Lance was the World Champion and the U.S. PRO Champion in road racing.
- In 1996, Lance was ranked the number one cyclist in the world.
- Lance was diagnosed with cancer in 1996. By 1998, he was back on his bike and winning races.
- Lance won the exhausting Tour de France race twice—in 1999 and 2000.
- Even though he had just recovered from a broken neck vertebra, Lance won a bronze medal at the 2000 Olympics in the time trials event.

PAOLA PEZZO

BIRTH DATE:
January 8, 1969
HOMETOWN:
Verona, Italy

Career Facts:

- Paola started cycling in 1989.
- In 1997, Paola won the World XC MTB Championships and the World Cup.
- Paola once rode 93 miles non-stop.
- In 1996, Paola won a gold medal in cross-country mountain biking at the Olympic Games. She defended her title and won the gold again at the Sydney Olympics in 2000.
- Paola rides 3 to 6 hours per day, seven days a week. She loves cycling up and down hills, and trains in the Alps every summer.

CHECK IT OUT

Read up on Lance Armstrong at

www.lancearmstrong.com

Pedaling to Fitness

Cycling is a demanding sport. It takes a lot of energy and endurance to ride a bike. Riders need to eat the right foods to keep their bodies fit for the challenge. A diet rich in vegetables, fruits, meats, breads and cereals, and milk and milk products is a great way to stay healthy. These tasty and nutritious foods provide bikers with important vitamins, minerals, protein, and fiber to keep their bodies at their best. Cyclists should also keep a water bottle with them on rides. They need to replace the water they lose through sweating while exercising.

Most fruits and vegetables are naturally low in fat and provide many nutrients important for health.

NORBA recommends that cyclists start drinking water 72 hours before a race to ensure that they are properly **hydrated**.

CHECK IT OUT

For more information on healthy eating, surf to
www.exhibits.pacsci.org/nutrition

Riders also need to keep their muscles in shape. Before hopping onto a mountain bike, riders should do a short warmup and then stretch well. Leg stretches, such as lunges and V-sits, are especially useful for cyclists. Keeping leg muscles supple helps prevent strains and injuries. Even after stretching well, riders do not start pedaling hard and fast. They begin slowly to get their bodies ready for action. During the winter, some cyclists visit their local gym and use the exercise bikes, or use other machines to keep fit.

Riding with friends is a great way to swap tips on how to look after a bike. It also gives riders the chance to try out other bikes.

Brain Teasers

How much do you know about biking? See if you can answer these questions!

Q Why do mountain bikers often wear tight-fitting clothing?

A Baggy clothing catches the wind and slows riders down. It may also get caught in the bike's machinery.

Q What is a tandem bicycle?

A A tandem is a bicycle built for two people. There are two seats, and two sets of pedals.

Q What does polo have to do with mountain biking?

A In bicycle polo, players on bikes use mallets to try to hit a ball through the other team's goal post.

Q How is a mountain bike seat different from a ten-speed or road bicycle seat?

A Mountain bicycle seats are wider and more comfortable. Riders travel over bumpy terrain, and a comfortable seat makes riding more enjoyable.

Q How long is the Tour de France road race?

A It is a twenty-five- to thirty-day race. Cyclists cover over 2,000 miles through France and Europe.

Q What difference do tires make?

A Fat tires slow riders down on smooth, hard surfaces. They are better for loose surfaces in off-road areas. Narrow tires are great for street riding.

23

Glossary

disqualified: not allowed to compete in a contest after breaking the rules

endurance: ability to survive hardship

faceplant: a crash where the rider falls over the handlebars

hydrated: having enough water in the body to keep it functioning correctly

precautions: safety measures

rugged: having an uneven surface; rough

sponsorship: money or products from a corporation or individual to fund an athlete

terrain: natural features of a stretch of land

titanium: a light, strong, silver-gray metal

traction: grip

treads: patterns in a tire for gripping

triathlete: an athlete who swims, bikes, and runs

velodrome: a stadium that has a banked track for bicycle races

Index

Web Sites

www.imba.com/kids/index.html

www.extreme.nas.net

www.wildgoose.com/mtbmain.htm

www.bmxtreme.com

www.lancearmstrong.com

www.exhibits.pacsci.org/nutrition

www.usacycling.org/corp/?documents/norba.html